The Nature Of Love

Romantic Muses and Images of Nature

By Lee Hiller

A Lee Hiller Nature of Love Book
LeeHiller.com

The Nature of Love

A Lee Hiller Nature of Love Book

This first on demand edition is made available
on the Internet in 2010

For more copies visit LeeHiller.com
Also available at Amazon.com

Contact me on Twitter @LeeHillerLondon
Become a Fan on facebook Hike Our Planet

Copyright ©2010 by Lee Hiller
All Rights Reserved

ISBN: 978-0-615-40970-2

"Love of nature is the essence of what is beautiful in mankind. Let your soul rejoice at even the smallest creature."
~ Lee Hiller

Table of Contents

Dedication 9
Forward 11
Introduction 13
    In Search of Love 13
    Learning Love to Love Myself 13
Wildflowers 17
    Wildflowers: Fuchsia Spiderwort 19
    Wildflowers: Lavender Oxalis 20
    Wildflowers: Wild Rose 21
    Wildflowers: Bird's-Footed Violet 22
    Wildflowers: Periwinkle 23
Wildlife 25
    Wildlife: Squirrel in the Ivy 27
    Wildlife: Cedar Waxwing 28
    Wildlife: Chipmunk 29
    Wildlife: Male Cardinal 30
    Wildlife: Black Swallowtail Butterfly 31
Rocks 33
    Rocks: Fire Red with Green Lichen 35
    Rocks: Blue and Amber with Gray Lichen 36
    Rocks: Amber Cream Silver Pewter Lichen 37
    Rocks: The Magic Rock Pool 38
    Rocks: Blue Gray Lichen Covered 39
Spring Blooms 41
    Spring Blooms: Saucer Magnolia 43
    Spring Blooms: Cherry Blossom 44
    Spring Blooms: Azalea 45
    Spring Blooms: White Dogwood 46
    Spring Blossoms: Red Tulip 47
Spring Leaves 49

- Spring Leaves: Pastels Pink and Green 51
- Spring Leaves: Spring Unfurls 52
- Spring Leaves: Life giving Rain 53
- Spring Leaves: The Birth of Spring 54
- Spring Leaves: Into the light 55

The Forest 57
- The Forest: Magic Fog 59
- The Forest: The Reflection 60
- The Forest: Spring Fog 61
- The Forest: Sunrise 62
- The Forest: Barely Spring 63

Nature's Details 65
- Nature's Details: False Turkey Tail Fungi Fans 67
- Nature's Details: Bumble Bee 68
- Nature's Details: Lichen 69
- Nature's Details: Hornet on Bird's-Foot Violet 70
- Nature's Details: Wooden Heart 71

Acknowledgements 73

"Thankful, Grateful, Blessed are easy words to say. Showing them silently via our actions touches the heart and soul." ~Lee Hiller

Dedication

I am dedicating my first book to my husband Rick London. Living with him I have learned the meaning of "True Love". A Love that can survive both the early flames of passion and the calm of respectful deep commitment to one and other. He has shared with me his love of humor, history, The US Constitution and poetry reopening my heart to the passion of words. Never wavering he supports my dreams without reserve and for this Love words seem inadequate.

Rick knows the disappointment of others not believing in your dreams. In the late 1990's his dream was to create an Off-Beat Cartoon series. He slept on the concrete floor of a metal warehouse struggling to make the pieces of his dream manifest into reality. To say I am proud of him would be an understatement, he is my hero. He dared to "Dream Big" and when others abandoned him he fought even harder to succeed. With the help of only a handful of friends and unexpected allies he did succeed, in 2010 Londons Times Cartoons (www.LondonsTime.us) celebrated its 13th Birthday. Today his "Off-Beat" cartoons can be found on products that are shipped daily throughout the world.

My Dearest Rick,

Your love has opened my heart and I have blossomed into the woman I always dreamed of becoming. I wake each morning filled with the excitement of loving you. At night I cannot sleep without hearing you whisper my name. My soul sings not alone but in the sweetest duet with yours. When I say I love you today it will pale in comparison to how I feel tomorrow.

I LOVE YOU BABY!
Your Lee xx00xx

"Our Love is so powerful it gave me the strength to cross a continent to be by your side. "
~ Lee Hiller

Forward

In this beautiful book, the nature of love and the love of nature embrace. Lee Hiller shares with us her very personal discovery of life's ultimate connection in poetic prose from the heart, and gives us all a glimpse of her daily delight in nature through photographs that wonderfully capture moments never to happen again, and yet that can inspire us over and over because of her artistic eyes and hands. It's at once both an intimate record of inner feeling, and a compendium of universal lessons for the spirit.

I'm blessed to know Lee, and Rick London – to whom the book is dedicated, and whose influence is so clearly on every page. They're both immensely creative and generous people. Their souls reach out and care for the world in many different ways each day. Their love for each other overflows onto these pages and offers inspiration for all who experience, or even aspire to, such exuberance of union in their own lives. And to any who doubt whether rapturous love for another human being, or for the small gifts of nature, is even possible in our time, this book serves as an ample demonstration that it is.

There are sentiments here, and images, that can spark extended reflection and meditation. Art and the poetry of the soul have always had that effect. In fact, you'll find your own images arising from the sentiments, and your own sentiments arising from the images – intensely personal thoughts will be coaxed from your heart by Lee's open sharing of hers, in both words and pictures.

Philosophers live in search of truth, beauty, goodness, and unity. You'll experience all four of these transcendental ideals reflected here. Allow them to enter your mind and heart. Then go and do your best to cultivate them anew in your life and your world.

Tom Morris

Dr. Tom V. Morris, PhD
 Philosopher and Author

Introduction

"When you least expect it Love finds you. Look not in places you would expect but venture out into the unknown. It is there you will be found and truly begin to live." ~ Lee Hiller

This is a book about Love, Love of another, Love of Nature and Love of Self. I have combined my daily Twitter Love muses for my Beloved Rick and my Love of sharing Nature via photography. It is my hope you will find Peace within my writing and photographs. Each page is an oasis of Love for you to experience alone or with someone you Love. Remember it is never too late to experience or express Love. You can follow us on Twitter @LeeHiller and @RickLondon we would Love to Tweet with you.

In Search of Love

"A passion for life was engulfing me and my soul soared high above as I drove, an awakening, a rebirth of my spirit." ~ Lee Hiller

For years I read the words of the greatest poets and philosophers longing to understand the love they described so eloquently. They appeared to chronicle love beyond the touch of mere mortals. Hearts and souls intertwined merging to become one. Lovers embracing now frozen in a moment for all eternity within a poem or sonnet. Just words, describing everything I wanted Love to be.

When Love finds you, Love as the poets described centuries past, do not look away. Give yourself over to its beauty and learn to trust your heart. Let go of fear and fall freely into your lover's arms. This is not just for the young renew your love with an affair of the heart. Remember those first days, months and years of being together.

Learning Love to Love Myself

"To be Love, give Love, accept Love, I Love myself without reservation or condition."
~ Lee Hiller

It sounds so simple, yet the important act of Loving ourselves is often never achieved. Like many woman I have struggled with body image, the aging process and relationship issues. In 2009 I began a journey of self discovery and fell in Love myself, gradually tossing out fifty-two years of accumulated baggage. I wanted to be free of the past, no longer looking back or living in the realm of the "What-If".

I began hiking in the Hot Springs National Park in November of 2009. The climb up the stairs and ramps to the promenade nearly did me in, looking up at the tower my first thought was about turning around. However the Mountain called so I climbed up the Tufa Terrace Trail, then on to the Peak Trail. The entire time I was huffing, puffing and thinking "Oh you old woman what were you thinking". I continued to the point where the Honeysuckle Tail branches off, bent over and threw up.

Feeling lighter I figured I would see if I could make it a little higher. So I decided to climb just a bit further, then one more bend and maybe another incline. Bent over huffing & puffing I looked up and in the distance saw the observation tower. I knew I would never forgive myself if I did not continue my climb to the top. This was pathetic and I was so happy I did not see anyone while I was gasping for air.

Still gasping and puffing I flung open the main doors to the tower like a survivor of an Alpine Plane crash looking for food and water. Once inside I realized the Tower was going to cost $7 and I did not bring any plastic. I poured my purse out on the counter and had exactly the $7 in bills and change. The Ride to the top was glorious and I began to forget the struggle to get there.

The climb to the tower turned out to be the catalyst, for the greatest change in my life. In the Forest Mountains of Hot Springs National Park I fell in Love with Nature and myself.

"If we cannot forgive others how can we forgive ourselves? If we do not Love ourselves how will we Love others?" ~ *Lee Hiller*

Love to You ALL,
Lee

The Nature Of Love

*"I am never lost in the mountains,
it is where I found myself."*

Wildflowers

*"I am a wildflower blossoming within
the gentle forest of our Love."*

Wildflowers: Fuchsia Spiderwort

"You are love and I give myself completely, without fear, letting go, falling freely into your embrace."

"One second in Love with you is an oasis in the storm of life."

"The heart of Love is unique within each soul. That any two come together to as one is a gift from the Universe."

"In our hearts lay silent truths revealed only in each other's embrace."

Wildflowers: Lavender Oxalis

"Love is the fuel that ignites my soul in the fire of our embrace."

"Our Love is an ocean, its tides rise and fall between our shores."

"You are your own best life coach; listen to your inner voice."

"From hearts and minds entwined arose a Love strengthened by the fire within our souls."

Wildflowers: Wild Rose

"Your smile illuminates my heart and is a joyous song for my soul."

"In your arms I melt to the warmth of your Love and the beauty of your soul."

"Lightly Love caresses our hearts speaking gently to our souls."

"You held me close when I needed you most cradling me in your infinite Love."

Wildflowers: Bird's-Footed Violet

"Your Love caresses my heart as softly as the wings of Angels."

"Our Love is never past or future it lives within each moment we are together."

"Your LOVE healed my heart and soul the first moment we touched."

"Sweet is the falling rain; each drop upon my skin reminds me of your Loving touch."

"I dream of Love and awaken each morning to its beauty wrapped in your arms."

Wildflowers: Periwinkle

"Through the storm your Love was a bright beacon leading me to your side."

"Lightening illuminates the sky as your Love does my heart, resonating through my soul."

"Love ignites a fire in our heart, lighting a journey of discovery for our Soul."

"Safely sleeping in the warmth of your Loving embrace I dance freely in my dreams."

Wildlife

"The beauty of any living creature can be seen with the soul."

Wildlife: Squirrel in the Ivy

"Love is often strong and fragile as it grows in the soil of our thoughts, words and deeds."

"When you Love yourself the Universe smiles."

"I am grateful for every lesson learned and humbled by those who give their time to teach me."

"Love is infinite and unique to each person's heart and soul."

Wildlife: Cedar Waxwing

"A thousand suns could not compare to the fire that burns in my heart for you."

"As sleep draws us in our bodies melt into each other in a bond of Love."

Wildlife: Chipmunk

"Your Love pierced my heart filling me with the light of hope and trust."

Wildlife: Male Cardinal

"Along each new trail your Love is with me as nature reveals herself."

"I am Love, desire, passion, hope, joy and peace when I am in your arms."

"In the glow of Our Love I am spirit, peace and one with all nature."

"As my spirit is set free by Nature's beauty my Love for You fills my soul."

Wildlife: Black Swallowtail Butterfly

"When we think love, breathe love, give love, the Universe loves us back."

"I find solace in your thoughts, peace in the way you speak my name
and contentment in the knowledge I am yours."

"When I awoke I was wrapped in the love you fill me with each night before I sleep."

"As I breathe in I love You as I exhale I love You."

I thank God every day that Love filled our hearts at the same moment."

Rocks

"As I walk with Nature my Love for you grows in each drop of rain and ray of sunlight."

Rocks: Fire Red with Green Lichen

"Your Love illuminates my heart casting out all shadows of the past."

"Paradise is wherever we are together."

"Look not skyward for Angels; they walk with Love and Strength upon this mortal plane."

"What wondrous moment could ever compare to the day you said "I Love You."

Rocks: Blue and Amber with Gray Lichen

"In your arms mortal barriers fade away as our souls dance in Love's sweet embrace."

"My heart burns in flames of Love when you proclaim I am yours."

"Dancing with me in the star filled sky, Love will lead as our souls soar above the earth."

"Within each kiss we share, life begins anew and Love is reborn."

Rocks: Amber Cream Silver Pewter Lichen

"I breathe in our Love as I lay my head against your chest and dreams unfold before me."

"The Light in my heart shines for you warming my soul."

"In your arms our Love's sweet song is a serenade to the Universe."

"Ecstasy is coming home and knowing I can slip into your embrace to hear the Universe sing."

Rocks: The Magic Rock Pool

"My Love rages in the confines of my heart, a torrent of desire bursting into an inferno of passion."

"The cool mountain air cannot pierce the warmth of our Lovers' embrace."

"Flirting with my Love is a sensual pleasure of the heart, passionate fire for the soul."

"Your warm embrace in silent slumber is a Love song to my soul."

Rocks: Blue Gray Lichen Covered

"When my mind met yours love blossomed and filled my soul.
Now I never feel empty or alone, you are with me."

"Dreams have given way to destiny; my life wrapped in your arms will soon be reality."

"To Love you and be Loved by you is gift of infinite beauty from the Universe."

"My soul has been set free by your Love and my heart bound to you for all eternity."

Spring Blooms

"Our Love is the spring, blossoming, renewing and growing in the warmth of each embrace."

Spring Blooms: Saucer Magnolia

"Your Love is morning sun as it warms my face in the cool mountain air."

"In your Loving arms dreams flow gently from my heart creating a visual feast for my soul."

"Love fills my dreams as I lay in your embrace softly sleeping to our souls serenade."

"Your breath against my neck as you whisper my name fuels Love's embers in my heart."

Spring Blooms: Cherry Blossom

"Our Love resonates in every breath, gesture, look, word and touch."

"LOVE is in your smile, first kiss of the day and the way you hold me as we sleep."

"Each breath I take fills me with our Love; each beat of my heart warms me with its fire."

"Traces of you linger on my skin, for your every touch is Love revealed."

Spring Blooms: Azalea

"Our Love is infinite within the Universe as it flows between our souls."

"Each touch and caress melts into me as a reflection of your Love."

"Your Love is in the rain as it washes over my body and the sun as it warms my skin."

"Your Loving touch heals the fractured pieces of my heart."

Spring Blooms: White Dogwood

"Your tender touch radiates Love's fire to my soul as I melt into your arms."

"My Love for you makes the coldest day of Winter feel like Spring."

"Love speaks softly within its power and strength."

"Your Love is the softly falling snow as it lightly caresses the earth."

Spring Blossoms: Red Tulip

"With a single touch I knew your Love was the promise of a life as one."

"You are everything my heart and soul desires, no other could pierce the Love I have for you."

"The warmth of the sun cannot compare to glow of your Love within me."

"In the darkness cool night air chills me, one whisper from your lips, I am on fire."

Spring Leaves

*"I dance lightly in your Love, swirling,
a leaf on the first Autumn breeze."*

Spring Leaves: Pastels Pink and Green

"Snow swirls softly around me, Nature's dance, lovingly caressing me."

"You are the sunlight as it rises to kiss the top of the trees in the early morning."

"Each smile and laugh you give to me is a Valentine that never leaves my heart."

"Our Love is in my heart, no matter how are far the trail leads me I will always return to you."

Spring Leaves: Spring Unfurls

"In the stillness of the mountain air I can hear the Universe sing our song of Love."

"Our Souls Dance to the Love song our hearts have discovered in each other's embrace. "

"In the Mountains our Love is renewed, like delicate Leaves awakening in the Spring."

"No woman could feel more Loved than I, in your embrace the Love of the Universe joins our souls."

Spring Leaves: Life giving Rain

"You fill my life with Love and Laughter, a potent tonic for the Soul."

"In the forest the morning sun warms my face, I close my eyes and you are here."

"Our Love is the spring, blossoming, renewing and growing in the warmth of each embrace."

"Dreams often stay locked in our hearts, your Love let mine out to play."

Spring Leaves: The Birth of Spring

"Your Love has taught my spirit to be free, I laugh, dance and play as Nature's child."

"Our Love makes the impossible, reality."

"In two Love grows making them one."

"No words are needed as you hold me; our bodies whisper I Love You in each other's embrace."

Spring Leaves: Into the light

"I willingly surrender to our love, falling freely into its embrace, serenity in knowing I am yours."

"To be near you, reveling in your closeness, you are my refuge, my Love."

"When your gaze caressed me I knew I would be yours forever."

"Bodies entwined, hearts beating as one, loving and being loved by you without hesitation or fear."

The Forest

*"In the forest the morning sun warms my face,
I close my eyes and you are here."*

The Forest: Magic Fog

"We soar free above the tree tops wrapped in the wings of our Love."

"Dance with me in the forest, caressed by the soft morning light, in the strong embrace of your Love."

"Hear our Love, it is the beat of that different drum, march, no dance with abandon to its rhythm."

"In Dreams or awake I do not fear the darkness for your Love illuminates my soul."

The Forest: The Reflection

"Dance with me in the rays of the sun, in the melting as one in glow of our Love."

"Your Love lifts my soul as gently as butterfly wings fluttering on a spring breeze."

"When I am with you my Love laughter fills my heart and ripples into the Universe."

"In the morning glow our Love caresses my heart and carries me deep into the forest."

The Forest: Spring Fog

"When I surrendered to our Love I lost nothing and gained everything."

"My soul sings a song in the forest, a serenade of the Love that burns in my heart for you."

"Our Love does not take sides; it pulls us to the middle, where Loving hearts live as one."

"My Love for you never waivers, I will walk beside you through all life's challenges."

The Forest: Sunrise

"Cradled, Caressed, Consoled in my hour of despair and pain Your LOVE carried me through."

"Come hike with me in the forest, in your arms under the blossoming trees is heaven."

"Your strength is the trees, your heartbeat the wind and your touch as the warmth of the sun on my skin."

"I heard your song in my heart and knew you spoke with Love, you were right."

The Forest: Barely Spring

"Air cannot sustain me, only the sound of love in your voice breathes life into me."

"When you whisper to me the song of our souls, its melody reverberates throughout the Universe."

"You are the light in my heart, the song in my soul and the embodiment of love. With you I am complete."

"I awaken my love, sweet dreams linger, ever sweeter from the warmth of you holding me close."

Nature's Details

"The Beauty of Nature is hidden within its smallest details."

Nature's Details: False Turkey Tail Fungi Fans

"A heart can bare its soul to the world and not be afraid when Loved."

"In you I have found Love; powerful, gentle and wise, it carries me to the mountain top."

"You are the golden morning sky warming my soul, filling my heart with desire."

"The mist on the mountains baths my soul in the renewal of our Love."

Nature's Details: Bumble Bee

"Let the breeze carry my Love to your heart, whispering sweet songs to your soul."

"Let the storm rage about us, in your arms our Love is a sweet surrender."

"In your Love I am set free, yet I cannot bear to leave your embrace."

"I dance in your Love, my heart soaring above the forest on a spring breeze."

Nature's Details: Lichen

"You are the warmth of the sand beneath my skin, your Love the ocean waves crashing into my body."

"Sweet surrender is in your arms, falling into our Love never wanting to stop."

"I have felt Love in the warmth of your gaze and been to heaven in the fire of your embrace."

"I have faith in you my Love; you are a gentle guiding soul cradling my heart."

Nature's Details: Hornet on Bird's-Foot Violet

"Each day we dance, lovers' hearts entwined, beating as one, keeping rhythm to our soul's serenade."

"Shadows of past pain are vanquished by your love when you whisper my name."

"Our love lingers softly upon me, caressing my heart, waiting patiently for the fire of our lovers embrace."

"When you made love to my mind my heart surrendered willingly to you and my soul was in ecstasy."

Nature's Details: Wooden Heart

"Our Love is a peaceful journey of the soul, serenity our hearts beating as one. "

"Your Love has freed me from living in the past; the present is heaven in your Loving arms."

"I am free in the glow of our Love, my soul rejoices as I melt into your embrace."

"Our Love is passions fire bathed in the calm of a deep commitment to each other."

Acknowledgements

I am blessed, humbled, and thankful for the many friends I have made on this journey. We sometimes want to believe we have done something alone, but in reality there are always people along the way who helped us to reach our goals and dreams.

I am blessed that my beloved Husband Rick London believed in me and my dream of reconnecting with Nature. I hike in the Mountains for hours each day seeking wisdom from the Forest and the many Creatures that call it home. Rick has always supported my hiking, writing and photography even though it meant I was away almost every morning. He spent hours, days and months helping me market my photographs, stepping way from his own work to teach me how to use many online design tools. Rick asked his product manufacturer to look at my work, this opened up another venue to showcase my photography and designs.

I was introduced to Tom Morris on Twitter by my then Fiancé' Rick. Tom's daily philosophy classes on Twitter encouraged me to open my mind to the wisdom of the past and apply it to my daily life. His wise counsel and friendship to both Rick and me is a gift beyond mere words. I am deeply grateful for the beautiful foreword he has written in this book.

Friends, it would be a lonely journey without them. I am thankful to have met so many wonderful people in the Mountains and online. Knowing you are venturing out with me on my hikes each day is a joy beyond words. Your generous encouragement has filled my heart with joy and I am forever grateful for your encouragement.

If you want to meet these wonderful people you can follow me on Twitter (@LeeHillerLondon) and or join Hike Our Planet on facebook.